Chaos P

CW00469345

Zaibah Iqbal

BookLeaf
Publishing

Presentation by *BookLeaf Publishing*

Web: www.bookleafpub.com

E-mail: info@bookleafpub.com

ISBN: 9789357440585

First edition 2023

To my late Grandmother Sakina and my late sister Zairah, whose names and my mother's memories bring warmth and joy to my soul.

ACKNOWLEDGEMENT

Thank you to: -

Allah - whom without, I would not be here.

Mum and Dad - who have supported me growing up and continue to embrace my eccentric self.

My sisters: Zainab, Zahrah and Zunairah - the Zsquad - for influencing and supporting my words, both spoken and unspoken.

My best friends, Saima and Firdos, who have seen it all and still love me for the wild child I can be.

To my secret loved ones - whom, without, my life would be strange.

PREFACE

I have always had trouble with expressing my emotions and I was never the type to keep a diary, but music and poetry were both my perfect allies in doing just that.

From every encounter in my life or by simple observations of people, I developed a sense of poetic dialect for every experience, and pretty soon realised poetry was my soulmate. Now I express myself, beautifully, on every page I can find; it's my liquid ambition.

Poetry, to me, is like writing a diary. Except, it's not always about me, and that's the best part about it.

If not now, then when?

It's never simple, is it?
The way your mind intertwines with mine.
And I want to run away.
From you, the truth, my own point of view.

But I stay, I'm awake.
My heart screams it's the wrong thing to do.

Another day and another dawn,
I'm falling apart inside.

Because there are holes in my soul,
And I can't move past my mind,
 - You're my subtle crime.

I fidget and flutter,
My heart stumbles and stutters.

Between reality and fantasy,
Craving all the things in my vicinity,
Seen as the sin in me.

But it's never simple, is it?
The way my time and my mind,
Are peaceful with you.

Yet, time is but forgotten,
When I'm hiding with you.

Kaleidoscope.

I spin around, deliriously, stuck in my thoughts
of you,
Your colours blinding my focus,
Intoxicated by the feeling of your rainbow shine
warming my soul,
Smooth against my face like a velvet paint
brush,
I happily lose sleep over you,
Smiling 24/7,
You are my kaleidoscope,
My dreamcatcher.

Powerful.

Run as fast as you can,
Run hard.

Pounding that energy into the ground.

Your neon tears on fire,
Igniting the pain.

This is your time,
Let it run its course.

It hurts. So bad.
Let it hurt. So bad.

Your drumming heart can take it,
Your burning breath is only temporary.

Drenched in sweat,
No one knows what you're feeling.

Don't compare yourself to them.

Your head and heart are your own,
Fight through the hardship.

Smear the neon tears away,
Make it your artwork.

Your canvas can be so beautiful,
If only you could see it.

There is power in your pain,
But you are powerful.

Sunshine.

Just after the rain has stopped pouring,
You know your place.

You save the day, but you're miles away,
So, how do you feel so close?

You stay awake when the moon's away,
The way you dazzle and shine,
I wish you were mine.

But you need your escape,
When the world is asleep,
So, you can safely rely on the moon.

To bring light to the dark,
To share your part,
And reflect on all that there is.

But it's nothing like you,
So warm, so true,
The moon is always in awe.

You occupy the sky like you occupy my mind,
And I know this feeling isn't new.

So, the next time you shine,
I'll call you mine,
And I'll leave my thoughts with the moon.

Because to be of your kind,
And to love you like you're mine,
Is something I know to be true.

You're the type.

You're the type of poetry I think too often about
to write,
Because when I first met you, I knew I was in
trouble.

But it hurts to know that you are real,
Because all I've ever known is how to be
something someone steals.

I was strong.
I was happiness.

She stole my strength.
She stole my happiness.

Until this day, I have never been the same,
Now you've walked in, and now I'm afraid.

Will things be different?
Will you be the same?

I am too lost in my heart to think with my head.

You told me about your girlfriend and you told
me about your pain.

I'm sorry about your girlfriend.
I'm sorry about your pain.

But if you plan on using me just to fulfil your
game,
I hope you walk away quietly for I will only
remember your name.

Last of us.

Your eyes behold dark mysteries,
Your lips define the night sky.

I am entangled in your enveloped emotions,
I am refusing to let go.

If I should walk away from you,
I fear I might fall,
Into the deep depths of your silvery soul.

High above the Fijian mountains,
Deep below the ocean's shore.

Come with me… will you?
Take my hand… in yours?

Maybe I am asking you for too much,
Maybe I should leave.

This is probably what you expected,
This is not what I planned to express.

I have spent too many long nights thinking too
much,

And have said too many meaningful sorries for
you to feel like they're hollow.

This goes above and beyond the I told you so's,
This goes above and beyond us.

This is you closing your eyes on me,
This is your lips remaining shut.

This is you always doubting me,
This is the last of us.

Blue.

Whenever I see the colour blue, it always
reminds me of you.
I'd sail the seas and ocean tides to find my way
to you.

Through a kaleidoscopic spectrum, my thoughts
are of different hues.
You ask me things I don't always know the
answers to, but I'll do my best for you.

"Blue shows me the colour of your bruises, and
the pain you tend to hide.
Let me offer you the colour of love and let it
heal your broken parts inside."

***

Months had passed since I last met you, and
winter has settled in.
I see you across the street, alone, and I wonder
how long it's been.

Blue fingers, blue lips, blue skies, blue kiss.
Every part of you, every part that I miss.

You've not changed at all, you're still beautifully you.
Yet my thoughts trace back to the time I last remembered you.

And when I asked you why you love blue so much,
You replied, "it's the opposite of you".

Expedition.

It's the way your hands slipped in from behind
and into my jacket,
And your hot breath tickled my ears but I didn't
mind.

Your cold fingertips traced my hot skin - like fire
and ice,
A chill ran up and down my spine.

I felt your soft eyes thinking and sighing,
Darting from your heart to mine.

I never seemed to get the message,
I never saw the signs.

It often seemed to sadden you,
When your thoughts I couldn't align.

I was happy you were here with me,
You were happy we were side by side.

We knew this wasn't going to last forever,
But we both knew that we would be fine.

Losing pieces.

I tried to change the stories when they started to sound like you.
I couldn't take the memories you left me with, I was starting to see the truth.
I got so lost in changing the description, but I still thought of you.
And when the memories started fading, and there was nothing I could do.
I tried to change it once again into something true.
And in that lovely process, I lost myself in you...

Supergirl.

You don't know me enough to know that my
darkest days aren't so dark anymore, or that the
rainbows I see are the most colourful than
they've ever been.

Don't take pity on me with only knowing my
past,
It's not the same anymore.

I'm capable of achieving good things too,
Just give me a chance and I'll show you.

If you're going to wait for me to make mistakes,
How am I supposed to have enough courage to
grow?

Believe in me.

Time can be of aid and pretty soon you will see,
Of all and everything I want to be.

I'll show you the Supergirl within me.

Saturday night rain.

It's finally the weekend,
I'm hoping you'll be free.

A chance for us to catch up,
A chance for you to talk to me.

I know you're busy with your family,
And I guess I am too.

But Saturday night rain feels different,
When I'm thinking about you.

Know your limits.

You broke the silence with the bitterness of your
words,
I guess some things are better left unsaid.

But you couldn't help yourself,
You had to have the last say.

Beautiful to brutal in an instance,
But always longing to fight for a battle that
wasn't yours.

Now you've gathered a line of enemies,
unexpectedly at your call,
Little did you know that the fights you fought,
didn't need your intrusions.

You made quite an entrance for them,
They could hardly forget you.

But you couldn't help yourself and I guess that's
why they say,
Some things are better left unsaid.

Ugh.

I am jealous of your confidence, and the way
you hold yourself.
You care about nobody, but claim nobody cares
about you as well.

But you so often criticise my demons, you so
often bid farewell.
I'll probably stay the same forever, trying to get
out of this manic hell.

I'm not good in keeping diaries, my pain is
worth more than this ink.
It's prayers and patience pushed together, forcing
me not to think.

About the lies I've painted golden and silver
linings that don't exist.
Precious time we wasted together, I just don't
know how I'll get over this.

Northern Lights.

I am drawn to you.
Like the night sky blanketed in its stars.
Your presence is of such magnitude.
I am in trepidation of your swirling rivers.

A connection so deep, so instinctive.
I can barely keep up with you.
But I stay awake to pursue your magic.
Dancing above the skyline, you are dangerous.

Your eyes, your silky waves, your ability to
obtain.
Hooked on your glow, I desire more.
But I marvel at our distance, it's safer this way.
Endless bounds of voices in desolate sync.

WTF?

it's like the stars kissed your face
- you're perfect.
does it hurt when you make a mistake?
- 100% chance of do-not-let-me-downs
would you hop over the moon with me, if it
meant happiness for you?
- sadness in your eyes has taught me that
happiness used to exist
don't do that, i was talking about you
- stubborn as an espresso aftertaste
i am leaving, you always do this
- leave a scar, i like scars
you make me laugh
- i? make? you? laugh?
tell me something stupid before I go to sleep
- i like to lick snowflakes

Tragic.

Damn, it's tragic.
When you start to lose you,
When you start to lose your magic.

Perhaps a little selfish.
But the thoughts in my mind,
They're not even mine.

I'm close to the edge.
But way beyond the surface,
A fingertip from coming out - alive.

A raging war, when they're keeping score,
Is this my freedom, or is there more?

June.

In the middle of June,
She walked in too soon.

With nothing but kindness,
And a handful of reminders.

A new face filling a new space,
She was healing me in her own ways.

My thoughts at times violent,
My feelings at times raw.

But her hugs they healed me,
And her love was so easy.

But in the middle of June,
When she walked in too soon?
She actually walked in at the perfect time.

Because she's sweet to the core,
She's someone I adore,
And I will always treat her like she's mine.

Silhouette.

Your silhouette, bright as a light,
- They just haven't met you yet.
Your stories told from young and old,
- Maybe we'll see you soon.
And strangers, they say, you were one for fame,
- But I think I would have known you better.

Your eyes, they shine, like sunsets and wines,
- The horizon would be so jealous.
Your words, so calm, as smooth as the seas,
- I hope you send a little prayer out for me.
Through lies, you disguise, your heart of gold,
- It's probably light as a feather.

Your friends, they're shy, when you pass them
by,
- Your presence is so special.
Your neighbours, they see, everything you
wished to be,
- In a town full of strangers.
But the people you please, are not worth your
appease,
- Spend time on what really matters.

So, keep your kindness, for the ones who need reminders,
- Of the people they could potentially be.
There's a whole world to explore, and your sisters will know,
- One day you will find your peace.

Rivers Edge.

It was like swimming in honey and rosé,
Something so beautiful yet so dangerous about
it.

Plunging deep into the horizon surrounding me,
Will life feel different once I'm through to the
other side.

Will I meet the one I've been searching for,
When I lost you once already.

Will you return to me.
- Be mine.

- But wait.
You look happier now.

What changed.
Something changed.

You've found someone new,
Someone more 'you'.

I used to wish for a brother.

I used to wish for a brother,
Just so I could play sports.

I used to wish for a brother,
So I could wear all the boyish clothes.

I used to wish for a brother,
So I could watch all the blood and gore,
From movies like Kickboxer to the iconic Die
Hard 4.

I used to wish for a brother,
But I don't wish for one anymore.

Because having three sisters,
Definitely means more.

Chaos.

Do they tell you about the feelings,
That grow when you're alone.

The ones as soft as seafoam,
And the ones as rough as stone.

They take shelter in your body,
And take some time with your soul.

But without all the chaos,
It just wouldn't feel like home.

Milton Keynes UK
Ingram Content Group UK Ltd.
UKHW020630070823
426447UK00017B/1079